EXPLORING THE WORLD

MITH

John Smith and the
Settlement of Jamestown

BY ROBIN S. DOAK

Content Adviser: Len Travers, Ph.D., Department of History,
University of Massachusetts, Dartmouth, Massachusetts

Reading Adviser: Dr. Linda D. Labbo, Department of Reading Education,
College of Education, The University of Georgia

COMPASS POINT BOOKS
MINNEAPOLIS, MINNESOTA

3109 West 50th Street, #115
Minneapolis, MN 55410

Visit Compass Point Books on the Internet at *www.compasspointbooks.com* or
e-mail your request to *custserv@compasspointbooks.com*

Photographs ©: Stock Montage, cover, 1, 24; North Wind Picture Archives, back cover (background), 8, 9, 13, 26, 27, 33, 34, 38; Hulton/Archive by Getty Images, 4, 10, 15, 17, 23, 25, 29; Richard T. Nowitz/Corbis, 5, 14, 30; Eric Crichton/Corbis, 7; Scala/Art Resource, N.Y., 11, 12; Courtesy National Park Service, Colonial National Historical Park, 16, 18, 19, 20; Bettmann/Corbis, 21, 31; NOAA, 35; Neil Rabinowitz/Corbis, 37; Giraudon/Art Resource, N.Y., 39; Nancy Carter/North Wind Picture Archives, 40.

Editors: E. Russell Primm, Emily J. Dolbear, Melissa McDaniel, and Catherine Neitge
Photo Researcher: Svetlana Zhurkina
Photo Selector: Linda S. Koutris
Designer: The Design Lab
Cartographer: XNR Productions, Inc.

Library of Congress Cataloging-in-Publication Data
Doak, Robin S. (Robin Santos), 1963–
  Smith : John Smith and the settlement of Jamestown / by Robin S. Doak.
      v. cm. — (Exploring the world)
  Includes bibliographical references and index.
  Contents: Excitement and exploration—A young adventurer—Setting sail for the new world—A legend is born?—Making Jamestown strong—Exploring New England—Final days.
  ISBN 0-7565-0423-6 (hardcover)
  1. Smith, John, 1580–1631—Juvenile literature. 2. Colonists—Virginia—Biography—Juvenile literature. 3. Explorers—America—Biography—Juvenile literature. 4. Explorers—Great Britain—Biography—Juvenile literature. 5. Jamestown (Va.)—History—17th century—Juvenile literature. 6. Jamestown (Va.)—Biography—Juvenile literature. 7. Virginia—History—Colonial period, ca. 1600–1775—Juvenile literature. [1. Smith, John, 1580–1631. 2. Explorers. 3. Jamestown (Va.)—History. 4. Virginia—History—Colonial period, ca. 1600–1775.] I. Title. II. Series.
  F229.S7D63 2003
  973.2'1'092—dc21   2002009924

Table of Contents

NOTE: In this book, words that are defined in the glossary
are in **bold** the first time they appear in the text.

Excitement and Exploration

From the age of sixteen, John Smith looked for adventure and excitement. Throughout his life, he played many roles. He was a soldier, a slave, and a pirate. His most important role, however, was as an explorer and a leader in North America. It was Smith's leadership that allowed Jamestown, the first permanent English settlement in North America, to survive. Without Smith's strict discipline and hard work, Jamestown might have failed.

Today, Smith is most famous for an event that might not even have taken place. It is said that a

John Smith was an important North American explorer and the savior of Jamestown.

*A reproduction of the Jamestown settlement where
Smith proved his leadership abilities*

young Powhatan Indian girl
named Pocahontas saved
Smith's life. She is supposed
to have kept her father from
having Smith put to death.

Through the years, doubts
about this story have overshad-
owed Smith's accomplishments.
Yet his contributions to the
early history and settlement

of the United States are clear. Smith's maps, letters, and books encouraged others to explore and to settle North America's Atlantic coast.

Some historians, or people who study the past, call Smith the father of the British colonies in North America.

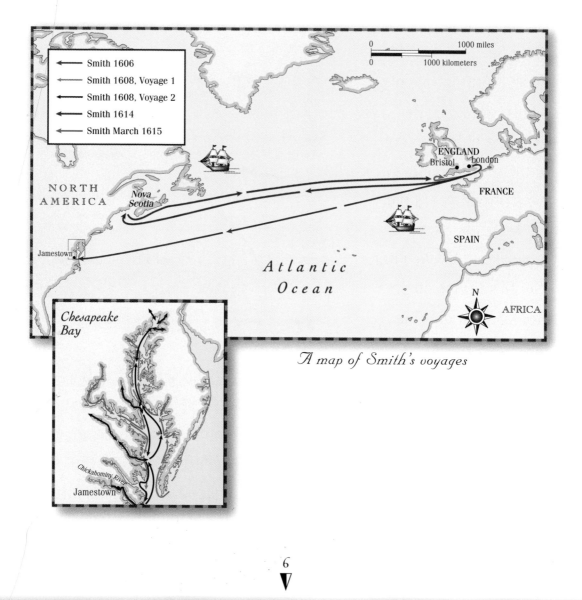

A map of Smith's voyages

A Young Adventurer

John Smith was born
in either late 1579 or
early 1580 in Lincoln-
shire, England. He
was the oldest son of
a farmer. When John
was fifteen years old,
he began working for
a **merchant**. A year later,
Smith's father died.
Young John quit his
job to travel the world
and find adventure.

During the next
ten years, Smith found
all the excitement he
could have imagined.

*Smith spent the first sixteen years of
his life in Lincolnshire, England.*

He first traveled to France. There he got his first taste of battle as a soldier for the French army. Smith also fought in Holland against the Spanish.

In 1600, Smith traveled to Hungary and Transylvania (now Romania) to fight against the Turks in what is known as the Long War. Smith became well known as an excellent soldier. He soon was pro-

Smith served with Dutch soldiers like this one while he was in Holland fighting against the Spanish.

moted to the rank of captain in the army. Over the years, many legends grew up around Smith. One of the earliest is from the time of the Long War. Smith reportedly battled three Turkish soldiers, one after another. As he defeated each soldier, he cut off the man's head and mounted it on a pike, or long spear. Then Smith

8

A woodcut depicting the legend of Smith (right) battling the third Turk

presented the heads to his commander. When the prince of Transylvania heard about Smith's actions, he rewarded him with some money. He also gave Smith a coat of arms, a banner with symbols for a particular person or family. The coat of arms given to Smith included an image of three heads that he had cut off during the war.

In November 1603, Smith fought the Turks in a huge, bloody battle. The Turkish army was so big that there were nearly four Turkish soldiers against every soldier in Smith's army. Smith's men were badly beaten. Smith himself was seriously wounded during the battle. He was unable to escape, and the Turks captured him. The Turks sold Smith into slavery and sent him to Constantinople (now

Smith's coat of arms showed the three heads of the defeated Turkish soldiers.

Istanbul) in Turkey. Later, Smith was shipped to another master, in Russia.

Smith's new master was cruel. He forced the young English-man to wear an iron collar, and often beat him. Smith later wrote about his life as a slave, saying it was a time that "a dog could hardly have lived to endure." Finally, Smith could not take it anymore. After one of the beatings, he killed his master with a club and escaped. Then he made his way across

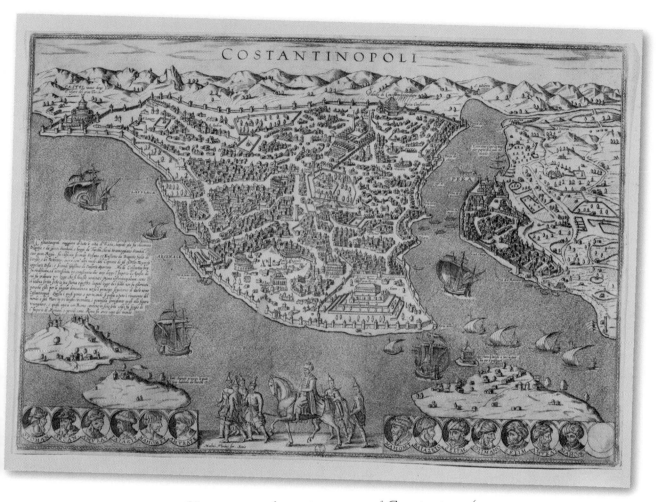

A seventeenth–century map of Constantinople

Russia on foot to Transylvania, where he found his troops.

In time, Smith was allowed to leave the army and was given a large reward for his service. Smith next began the long journey home. Before finally arriving back in England in 1604,

Smith traveled through Africa before returning to England.

he traveled throughout Europe and Africa. At the age of twenty-five, Smith was an experienced soldier and world traveler. He had fought in battles and been made a slave. Yet Smith's life of adventure and excitement was just beginning.

Setting Sail for North America

Smith spent the next year in England, but he soon grew bored. By 1606, he was in London, England, looking for a new adventure. It was there that he learned of the Virginia Company of London.

King James I of England had given the Virginia Company permission to set up colonies in North America. The company's founders believed they would find silver and gold there. Their goal was to send people to the area called Virginia to find these riches. The company also hoped that the settlers would discover the **Northwest Passage,** a supposed water route across

England's King James I

A replica of the Susan Constant *is docked at Historic Jamestown.*

North America that many believed existed.

Smith gave money to the Virginia Company. He also decided to become involved with the company's new settlement. On December 20, 1606, Smith was one of 105 men and boys who boarded three ships headed to Virginia. The *Susan Constant,* the *Godspeed,* and the *Discovery* sailed for four months before reaching the Virginia coast.

During the voyage, Smith was accused of **mutiny.** Some

believed that he planned to make himself king of the new settlement once they arrived. Smith spent the rest of the journey locked in chains. At one stop during the voyage, those in charge even built **gallows** to hang him on. However, Smith later wrote, he "could not be perswaded [convinced] to use them."

The ships finally reached Virginia on April 26, 1607. Smith was impressed with his first sight of North America. "Heaven and earth never agreed better to frame a place for man's **habitation,**" he wrote. Another settler agreed, writing

Upon landing in Virginia, many of the settlers were impressed with what they saw.

about the region's beautiful meadows and tall trees.

Before going ashore, the settlers opened a locked box that Virginia Company officials had sent on the trip. The box held the names of seven men who had been chosen in advance to govern the new colony. Many of the settlers were shocked when they saw John Smith's name on the list. They refused to allow Smith to take his rightful place on the colony's governing council.

The three ships traveled 60 miles (97 kilometers) up the James River before they found a spot for their settlement. They named it Jamestown, in

Jamestown was built in a swampy area that proved unhealthy.

Native Americans inhabited the land around Jamestown.

honor of King James I. It was the first permanent English settlement in North America. Unfortunately, the settlers chose a bad site for Jamestown. They built it on a swampy, mosquito-infested patch of land with no clean drinking water nearby.

Even worse, the settlement was located on land belonging to the **Powhatan Confederacy**. This was a group of about thirty Native American tribes in the Virginia area. In the coming years, the people of Jamestown would have many problems with their Powhatan neighbors. Many of the Native Americans believed that the settlers had no right to live on their land.

Smith thought that the settlers should build a strong fortress to protect Jamestown from Native American attacks. The council leaders disagreed. They decided to build a small wooden fence. On May 26, 1607, two hundred Powhatan warriors attacked the settlement. They killed two people and wounded ten others before being scared away by cannon fire. After the attack, the

The settlers followed Smith's advice and began building a stronger fort after they were attacked by Native Americans.

Smith established trade with the Native Americans.

colonists built a stronger fort and welcomed Smith onto the governing council.

Smith spent his first few months in North America exploring the Virginia area. He met with Native Americans and began trading with them. He even began to learn the language spoken by the local Native Americans. By the summer, Smith was the settlement's chief trader.

In June, the three ships set sail for the return trip to England. Life quickly became more difficult for the people who stayed in Jamestown.

Many colonists had to bury friends who died during the first hard winter at Jamestown.

From June to September, about fifty men died. Many more were weakened by disease.

By winter, the settlers were in trouble. They lived in simple houses with walls of clay that barely kept out the cold. They had little food or fresh water. Ships from England would not arrive with supplies and new settlers until the following April. By then, only 38 of the original 105 colonists would be alive to greet them.

A Legend Is Born?

D During that first brutal winter, Smith searched for food and supplies. In December 1607, he and two other men set out by boat up the Chickahominy River. When they landed, they were attacked by a group of Powhatan Indians. The Powhatans took Smith prisoner and killed his companions.

Smith fought with the Powhatans during his journey up the Chickahominy River.

Smith was brought before the Native Americans' leader. His name was Wahunsonacock, but he was known to the English as Powhatan. Powhatan headed the Powhatan Confederacy. After questioning Smith, Powhatan ordered that the stranger be put to death.

Two Powhatan warriors grabbed Smith. They forced him to his knees and made him lay his head on two large stones. Then they raised their clubs and prepared to smash his head.

At the last moment, Powhatan's young daughter stepped in. Her name was Mataoka, but she was nicknamed Pocahontas. Smith later wrote, "The Kings dearest daughter . . . got [my] head in her armes, and laid her owne upon [mine] to save [me] from death." The chief agreed to spare Smith's life. He later declared that he and the Englishman were friends. Smith returned to Jamestown with food for the settlers, supplied by Powhatan and his tribe.

Where did this story come from? Smith himself wrote about it in a book he published in 1624. At first, no one questioned the story. In the mid-1800s, however, historians began to doubt Smith's story. They pointed out that he never talked about the event until many years after it was supposed to have happened.

*Smith claimed that Pocahontas convinced
her father to spare his life.*

Pocahontas was a friend to the Jamestown colonists.

Some people thought Smith bragged and was therefore unable to re-tell stories truthfully. As a result, Smith was labeled a liar.

In recent years, historians have looked more closely at Smith's story. Some believe that he was indeed telling the truth. Whether or not the event took place, Pocahontas later played an important role in helping James-town's early settlers. Smith said that she often brought food to the settlers.

Making Jamestown Strong

When Smith returned to Jamestown, the council placed him under arrest. He was tried for causing the deaths of the two men with him who had been killed. Smith was found guilty and was sentenced to be hanged. Luckily, Smith was spared, and supply ships soon arrived from England,

Henry Hudson, Smith's friend and a fellow explorer

bearing food and new settlers. When the supply ships returned to England, they carried letters from the settlers. One letter was from Smith to his friend Henry Hudson. It told Hudson about the possibility of finding a Northwest Passage somewhere along the Atlantic coast of North

America. It also contained a map of the area to help Hudson search. Hudson used his friend's letter and map to convince his crew to explore the coast in 1609. During that trip, Hudson claimed what became known as the Hudson River region for the Dutch.

Smith also sent home a handwritten copy of his first book. It was called *A True* *Relation of Such Occurrences and Accidents of Noate as Hath Hapned in Virginia since the First Planting of That Collony.* The book was printed in England and sold well, making Smith famous.

During the summer of 1608, Smith set out again to explore the region. On one trip, he explored the Chesapeake Bay area. During that trip,

Smith (standing, far right) explored Chesapeake Bay in 1608.

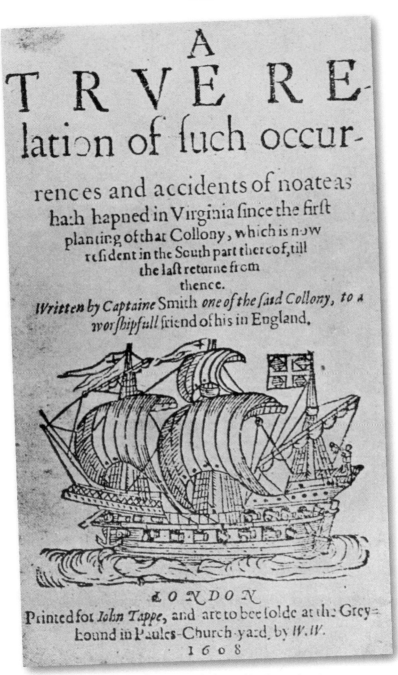

A TRVE RElation of such occurrences and accidents of noateas hath hapned in Virginia since the first planting of that Collony, which is now resident in the South part thereof, till the last returne from thence.

Written by Captaine Smith *one of the said Collony, to a worshipfull* friend of his in England.

LONDON

Printed for *John Tappe,* and are to bee solde at the Greyhound in Paules-Church-yard, by *W.W.*

1608

The title page of Smith's first book

Smith and others sailed as far north as present-day Baltimore, Maryland. They also journeyed up the Potomac River to present-day Washington, D.C. Smith's map of the area was accurate, well-drawn, and filled with detail. It would be used for many years to come.

Smith knew what needed to be done to make the settlement successful. In September, he was chosen to be the new president of Jamestown's governing council. He told the people of Jamestown to stop searching for gold. Then, using threats and strict discipline, Smith ordered the men to work hard so Jamestown would survive. Each man was required to work six hours each day.

Smith warned, "He that will not worke shall not eat." Smith was true to his word: Those who refused to do their share were left to starve on the other side of the James River.

Smith himself was not afraid to get his hands dirty. He farmed, cut logs, built houses, and did whatever was needed to make the settlement successful. He made the fortress stronger and safer. He encouraged the men to fight if the Powhatans attacked Jamestown.

During Smith's time as leader of Jamestown, the settlers fared well. His strength and toughness were exactly what the settlement needed to survive. Thanks to Smith's

Colonists eventually gave up searching for gold and began performing more practical tasks, such as making bricks.

leadership, the colonists were able to keep from starving.

Then, in September 1609, Smith was badly burned when a spark lit his gunpowder bag on fire. Smith was put on a

When Smith set sail for England in 1609, he didn't know it was the last time he'd see Virginia's shores.

ship and sent back to England to heal. Smith did not know it, but this was the last time he would ever see Virginia, the colony he had helped to establish.

Exploring New England

Smith suffered terribly during the long voyage back to England. When the ship arrived in London in December 1609, Smith was told that the Virginia Company would not pay his wages. Instead, the company charged him with doing a bad job of managing the Jamestown settlement.

Back in London, Smith took up his pen and wrote about his time in North America. Over the next twenty years, he

THE
TRUE TRAVELS,
ADVENTVRES,
AND
OBSERVATIONS
OF
Captaine IOHN SMITH,
In *Europe, Asia, Affrica,* and *America,* from *Anno Domini* 1593. to 1629.

His Accidents and Sea-fights in the Straights; his Service and Stratagems of warre in *Hungaria, Transilvania, Wallachia,* and *Moldavia,* against the *Turks,* and *Tartars;* his three single combats betwixt the *Christian* Armie and the *Turkes.*

After how he was taken prisoner by the *Turks,* sold for a Slave, sent into *Tartaria;* his description of the *Tartars,* their strange manners and customes of Religions, Diets, Buildings, Warres, Feasts, Ceremonies, and Living; how hee slew the Bashaw of *Nalbritts* in *Cambia,* and escaped from the *Turkes* and *Tartars.*

Together with a continuation of his generall History of *Virginia, Summer-Iles, New England,* and their proceedings, since 1624. to this present 1629; as also of the new Plantations of the great River of the *Amazons,* the Iles of S.t *Christopher, Mevis,* and *Barbados* in the *West Indies.*

All written by actuall Authours, whose names you shall finde along the History.

LONDON,
Printed by *F. H.* for *Thomas Slater,* and are to bee sold at the Blew Bible in *Greene Arbour.* 1630.

Smith was both a famous explorer and an early travel writer.

would become North America's first travel writer. Smith's books and maps encouraged others to settle the continent. His books include *The Generall Historie of Virginia, New-England, and the Summer Isles* (1624) and *The True Travels, Adventures, and Observations of Captaine John Smith in Europe, Asia, and Africa, and America* (1630).

In the books, Smith told future settlers what was needed to survive in North America. One book even included a checklist of items that colonists should bring with them. Items on the list included three shirts, four pairs of shoes, twelve needles, a gallon of brandy, a suit of light armor, a long gun, a sword, ten hoes, seven axes, and two hammers.

By 1614, Smith was ready for more adventure. He wanted to return to North America, but he did not want to go back to Virginia. This time, Smith hoped to explore "Northern Virginia," the territory north of Jamestown. He was most interested in an area that he later named "New England."

It took time, but Smith was finally able to find sponsors—people to pay for his voyage of exploration. The sponsors hoped that Smith would find gold and other riches during his journey. They allowed him to use two ships, the *Frances* and the *Queen Anne.* Smith loaded the ships with supplies and

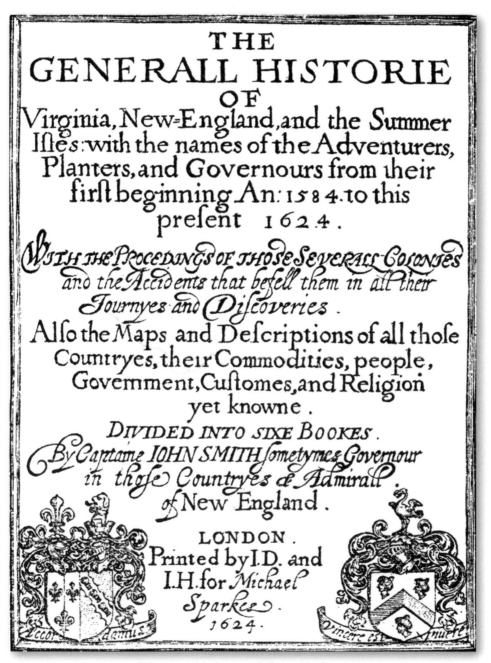

THE
GENERALL HISTORIE
OF
Virginia, New=England, and the Summer
Isles: with the names of the Adventurers,
Planters, and Governours from their
first beginning An: 1584. to this
present 1624.

With the Procedings of those severall Colonies
and the Accidents that befell them in all their
Journyes and Discoveries.

Also the Maps and Descriptions of all those
Countryes, their Commodities, people,
Government, Customes, and Religion
yet knowne.

DIVIDED INTO SIXE BOOKES.

By Captaine IOHN SMITH sometymes Governour
in those Countryes & Admirall
of New England.

LONDON.
Printed by I.D. and
I.H. for Michael
Sparkes.
1624.

The cover of one of Smith's books

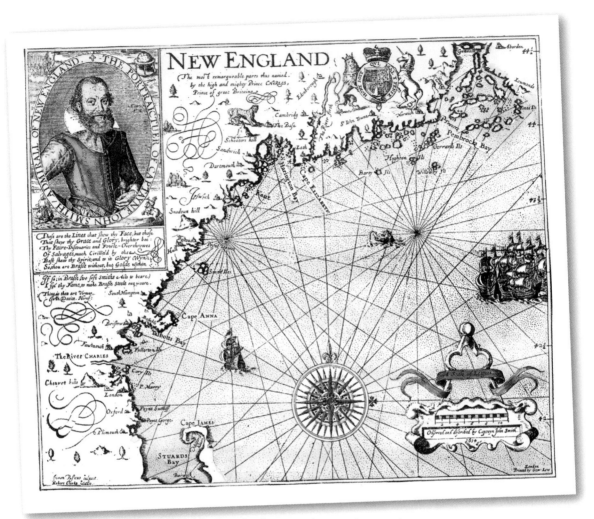

*Smith sketched maps during his exploration
of North America's Atlantic Coast.*

fishing and whaling gear. In early March, the ships left England for North America.

Once the ships arrived off the coast of Maine, the sailors began fishing. During this trip,

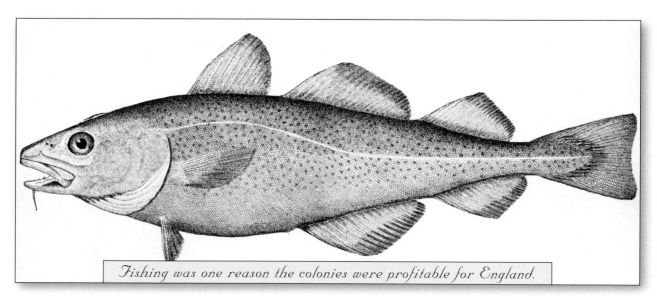

Fishing was one reason the colonies were profitable for England.

Smith and eight or nine other men explored the coast. Smith sketched the coastline from what is now Nova Scotia to Rhode Island. The maps that were made from these sketches would be very important to people journeying to the region.

When Smith returned to England in August, he did not have the gold and other riches that his sponsors had hoped for. His ships, however, were filled with other valuable items, including furs, dried fish, and fish oil. The sponsors sold these goods for a large profit. Smith's journey proved that the colonies could make money for England.

Final Days

Back in England, Smith thought of his biggest idea yet: He would sail to New England and start a colony there. During the time he had spent exploring Virginia and New England, Smith had gained valuable knowledge. He knew that he would need hard workers to set up a successful settlement.

Smith considered a number of sites for his new settlement. They included present-day Boston; Plymouth, Massachusetts; and Portsmouth, New Hampshire. Before sailing, however, it seems that Smith decided to establish his new colony somewhere in Maine.

In March 1615, Smith and sixteen would-be colonists set sail for New England. When they were still less than 200 miles (322 km) from England, however, a huge storm swelled up. The fierce winds battered Smith's ship. He was forced to turn around and head back to England.

In June, Smith and his colonists set sail again. The ship was attacked by French

Before setting sail in 1615, Smith decided
to set up his new colony in Maine.

Smith and his crew faced an attack by French pirates.

pirates, and Smith was taken prisoner. He spent months on board the French pirate ship. He even took part in some raids on Spanish ships. During that time, Smith wrote another book, which he called *A Description of New England.* Eventually, Smith was able to steal a small boat and escape.

He returned to England but could not convince anyone to pay for his next trip. Smith claimed that he offered to go with the Pilgrims to North America, but they said no.

Smith was not among the Pilgrims who arrived in Plymouth, Massachusetts, in 1620.

John Smith is remembered for his courageous exploration of North America and his wise leadership of the Jamestown settlement.

In 1622, he offered to return to Virginia to help organize an army to fight the Powhatan Confederacy. Again, he was refused.

For the next nine years, Smith continued to write books. He also waited for the chance to return to North America.

As late as 1630, he offered his services to colonists in Massachusetts. "I am ready to live and dye among you," he wrote. On June 21, 1631, the man known for his adventurous spirit and his many travels died at home in London, England. He was fifty-one years old.

Glossary

colonies—territories settled by people from other countries and controlled by those countries

gallows—a frame used to hang a person

habitation—a place to live

merchant—someone who sells goods for profits

mutiny—a rebellion aboard a ship

Northwest Passage—a sought after water route believed to exist across North America, connecting the Atlantic and Pacific Oceans

Powhatan Confederacy—a group of about thirty Native American tribes in the Virginia area in the 1600s

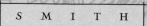
Did You Know?

∾ John Smith almost died in 1608 while exploring the Rappahannock River in Virginia. During a fishing expedition, he was stung by a stingray, a sea animal with a poisonous spine on its tail. Fortunately, he survived and ended up eating the stingray. The area is now known as Stingray Point.

∾ When Smith reported on the conditions in the Chesapeake Bay area, he depicted waters teeming with fish. He said there were trees so large that a canoe could be made from only one of them and still manage to hold forty men.

∾ Once he returned home for good, Smith was visited in England by Pocahontas (known to the English as Lady Rebecca) and her English husband, John Rolfe.

∾ Even though many historians consider Smith a hero, many think he was conceited and allowed bragging to get in the way of describing historical events accurately.

Important Dates in Smith's Life

c. 1579

Smith born in Lincolnshire, England

1607

Smith arrives in Virginia and begins work on the Jamestown settlement; during the winter, the colony is severely lacking in food and supplies

1614

Smith maps the stretch of coast from Nova Scotia to Rhode Island

1608

Smith explores the Chesapeake Bay area

1631

Although he says he would have been happy to spend his last days among British colonists in North America, Smith dies at home in London

1600–1604

Smith gains fame fighting the Turks in Eastern Europe

Important People

HENRY HUDSON (C.1565–?) John Smith's friend and a fellow explorer; Smith told Hudson the Northwest Passage might be located along the Atlantic coast of North America, and Hudson became famous for his exploration of that region in 1609

KING JAMES I (1566–1625) English king who gave the Virginia Company permission to set up colonies in North America

POCAHONTAS, ALSO KNOWN AS MATAOKA (c.1595–1617) daughter of Powhatan and the person supposedly responsible for sparing Smith's life when he was taken hostage by her people; she later became friends with Smith, married Englishman John Rolfe, and moved to England

POWHATAN, ALSO KNOWN AS WAHUNSONACOCK (c.1545–1618) leader of the Powhatan Confederacy and the father of Pocahontas

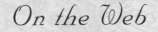

Want to Know More?

At the Library

Edwards, Judith. *Jamestown, John Smith, and Pocahontas in American History.* Springfield, N.J.: Enslow, 2002.

Foster, Genevieve. *The World of Captain John Smith.* Sandwich, Mass.: Beautiful Feet Books, 1999.

Kline, Trish. *Captain John Smith.* Vero Beach, Fla.: Rourke Publishing, 2002.

On the Web

John Smith
http://www.zoomdinosaurs.com/explorers/page/s/smith.shtml
For a short biography of Smith

John Smith History
http://www.seacoastnh.com/johnsmith/links.html
For a biography and links

The Writings of Captain John Smith
http://www.members.aol.com/mayflo1620/smith_writings.html
For letters and other writings by John Smith

Through the Mail

Jamestown Rediscovery

1367 Colonial Parkway
Jamestown, VA 23081
To view exhibits related to the remains
of the Jamestown settlement

On the Road

Flowerdew Hundred Museum

P.O. Box 1624
1617 Flowerdew Hundred Road
Hopewell, VA 23860
804/541-8897
To learn about one of the earliest land grants
in Virginia and view artifacts of this working
farm dating from 1619

Index

About the Author

Robin S. Doak has been writing for children for more than fourteen years.
A former editor of *Weekly Reader* and *U*S*Kids* magazine, Ms. Doak has
authored fun and educational materials for kids of all ages. Some of her
work includes biographies of presidents such as John Tyler and Franklin D.
Roosevelt, as well as other titles in this series. Ms. Doak is a past winner
of an Educational Press Association of America Distinguished Achievement
Award. She lives with her husband and three children in central Connecticut.